Armentrout, David

Gibbons

Gibbons

David and Patricia Armentrout

Rourke
Publishing LLC
Vero Beach, Florida 32964

www.rourkepublishing.com

PHOTO CREDITS: Cover © David C. Rehner; title page © Allen Nevalainen; pg. 04 © PhotoDisc; pg. 05 © Robert Adrian Hillman; pg. 06 © Eun Jin Ping Audrey; pg. 07 © Winter Witch; pg. 09 © Peter Short; pg. 10 © Micha Fleuren; pg. 11, 12 © Gary Unwin; pg. 13 © Timothy Craig Lubcke; pg. 15 © Simone van denBerg; pg. 16 © Phil Morley; pg. 17 © Kabir Bakie; pg. 18 © Robert Adrian Hillman; pg. 19 © Henry Williams Fu; pg. 20 © Raul; pg. 21 © Michael Hare; pg. 22 © Martina Berg;

Editor: Robert Stengard-Olliges

Cover design by: Nicola Stratford, bdpublishing.com

Library of Congress Cataloging-in-Publication Data

Armentrout, David, 1962-
  Gibbons / David and Patricia Armentrout.
    p. cm. -- (Amazing apes)
  ISBN 978-1-60044-566-8
  1. Gibbons--Juvenile literature. I. Armentrout, Patricia, 1960- II. Title.
  QL737.P96A754 2008
  599.88'2--dc22
                          2007011867

Printed in the USA

CG/CG

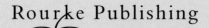

Rourke Publishing

www.rourkepublishing.com – rourke@rourkepublishing.com
Post Office Box 3328, Vero Beach, FL 32964

Table of Contents

Gibbons

Gibbons are small, slender **primates** like monkeys and great apes. There are many **species** of gibbons. They share many traits with great apes, but because gibbons are smaller they are called lesser apes.

  Gibbons have thick hair that ranges from light colored to dark brown or black. They have very long arms and can easily grasp things with their hands and feet. Like gorillas, orangutans, and chimps, gibbons do not have tails.

Home in the Trees

Gibbons live in the tropical rainforests of Southeast Asia. They are **arboreal**, which means they spend most of their time in trees. Gibbons do not build nests like other apes. Instead, they sleep upright in a fork of a tree branch, alone or huddled with family members.

East China Sea

Gulf of Tonkin

ASIA

South China Sea

Andaman Sea

Gulf of Thailand

Strait of Malacca

■ **Gibbon Habitat**

Sulu Sea

Celebes Sea

Molucca Sea

Java Sea

9

Indian Ocean

Flores Sea

Daily Life

Gibbons are **omnivores**. They eat fruits, leaves, small buds, insects, and sometimes bird eggs and small birds.

Gibbons can walk across large branches. They use their arms for balance.

Social Animals

Gibbons are very social animals. They communicate with body movements and vocals. Gibbons use calls to attract mates, to warn other gibbons of danger, and to defend their territory.

Each morning a female gibbon will begin her call,
and then her mate will join in. They both create a loud,
long song in the forest trees. Their song may last
30 minutes.

Together they warn other gibbon families not to approach the fruit in their trees.

Gibbons live
25 to 30 years in the wild
and as long as 40 years
in captivity.

Lar Gibbons

Gibbons weigh 12 to 50 pounds (5 to 22 kilograms) depending on the species. The Lar gibbon is the smallest gibbon species. Lar gibbons have a dark face trimmed in white, and white hands and feet. Lar gibbons are also called whitehanded gibbons.

The Siamang

Siamangs are the largest of the gibbon species. They have a dark face, black fur, and two of their toes are fused together on each foot. They are the loudest of all the gibbons.

Gibbons in Danger

Gibbons are the acrobats of the rainforest. But their highflying antics don't always keep them safe. Some people hunt them for food, catch and sell them, and destroy their rainforest home. Fortunately, many other people work to protect and save gibbons from **extinction**.

Glossary

arboreal (ar BOR ee ul) — living in trees

extinction (ek STINK shun) — no longer existing

omnivores (OM nih vorz) — animals that eat plants
 and meat

primates (PRY maytz) — a group of intelligent animals
 that includes monkeys, apes, and humans

species (SPEE seez) — a kind of animal

Index

FURTHER READING

Ingebretsen, Karen. *Gorillas and Other Apes*. World Book Inc., 2005.

Taylor, Barbara. *Apes and Monkeys*. Kingfisher, 2004.

Sjonger, Rebecca. *Monkeys and Other Primates*. Crabtree Publishing, 2006.

WEBSITES TO VISIT

www.enchantedlearning.com/subjects/apes/gibbon/

www.gibboncenter.org/

nationalzoo.si.edu/Animals/Primates/

ABOUT THE AUTHOR

David and Patricia Armentrout have written many nonfiction books for young readers. They have had several books published for primary school reading. The Armentrouts live in Cincinnati, Ohio, with their two children.